PEOPLES KOREA SMASHES COUNTER-REVOLUTION

INTRODUCTION
The exposure ,defeat and the liquidation of the anti-party counter-revolutionary factional clique in the DPRK was a great victory as the scenario that the imperialists and revisionist traitors had mapped out for the DPRK was smashed and counter-revolution stopped dead in its tracks.

We in the Juche Idea Study Group of England , the Association for the Study of Songun Politics UK and the UK Korean Friendship Association we never had any truck with those false friends of the DPRK who seek "build bridges " into the DPRK in order to promote "reform" and "opening up " , in other words the restoration of capitalism in the northern part of Korea.

The most dangerous enemy a country can face is the enemy within, the unseen hidden enemy that smiles at your face while hiding a dagger behind the back . Peoples Korea of Juche under the Songun-based revolutionary leadership of supreme leader Marshal Kim Jong Un has decisively smashed the internal enemy , the class enemy . Former socialist countries failed to do so.

People's Korea smashes counter-revolution-special article by JISGE and ASSPUK chairman

The dear respected leader Marshal KIM JONG UN guides meeting of WPK Politburo

Rubbish ejected from meeting.

Recently, on the 8th of December an enlarged meeting of the Political Bureau of the Workers' Party of Korea was held under the guidance of dear respected Marshal Kim Jong Un the First Secretary of the WPK . At the meeting the crimes of the counter-revolutionary anti-party factional clique of traitor Jang Song Thaek were laid bare so the meeting decided to remove Jang from all of his positions and expel him from the party.

Jang is a counter -revolutionary criminal who schemed in a most two-faced manner to restore capitalism in the DPRK and make the DPRK either a colony of the US or a satellite state of a certain big power. Jang had been sabotaging parts of the DPRK independent national economy over a period of time, even selling off the resources of the DPRK at a low price and disrupting the production of Juche steel, Juche fertiliser and Juche vinalon . Furthermore as the KCNA report of the December 8th Political Bureau of the WPK says

" *The Jang group weakened the party's guidance over judicial, prosecution and people's security bodies, bringing very harmful consequences to the work for protecting the social system, policies and people.*

Such acts are nothing but counter-revolutionary, unpopular criminal acts of giving up the class struggle and paralyzing the function of popular democratic dictatorship, yielding to the offensive of the hostile forces to stifle the DPRK." (KCNA)

The struggle for building socialism is always accompanied by a fierce class struggle in which there can be no compromise or concession .

Jang was clearly a capitalist-roader " who *Affected by the capitalist way of living, Jang committed irregularities and corruption and led a dissolute and depraved life.*"(KCNA)

The DPRK has a proud history of class struggle , a struggle against counter-revolutionary elements . During the fierce Fatherland Liberation War(Korean war) the Pak Hong Yon-Li Sung Yop spy clique who were agents of the US imperialist Central Intelligence Agency betrayed the country , caused losses in the war and planned to overthrow the leadership. The great revolutionary leader generalissimo Kim Il Sung smashed them and saved the DPRK from being sold out to US imperialism and turned into a colony of the US. In 1956 when modern revisionism reared its ugly head in the international communist movement a factional clique planned to overthrow the supreme leadership of the DPRK and declare Korea a pro American 'neutral nation' . The great leader comrade Kim Il Sung exposed and defeated these factionalists and went deep amongst the people and got their support.

The workers in the Kangson Steel Plant told Kim Il Sung that if the factionalists were sent to them, they would throw them into the electric furnace, and a granny in Taesong Village told him; *"Premier, after all, it's we who will win, and not the factionalist rogues, you see? Don't worry. We support you."* These were expressions of the steely conviction and will of the entire people of the country. Through the struggle against factionalism the purity of the Party ranks was secured all the more, and the unity and cohesion of the Party and revolutionary ranks was made unbreakable.

Now the counter -revolutionary Jang Song Thaek faction have tried to overthrow to destroy the DPRK from within and restore capitalism . However their exposure , defeat and purge is most timely. Dear respected Marshal Kim Jong Unhas struck a telling blow at them. This shows the great intelligence and foresight of dear respected Marshal Kim Jong Un who is following in the footsteps of the great leaders generalissimo Kim Il Sung and generalissimo Kim Jong Il.

Other socialist countries were not so fortunate as the DPRK . In the Soviet Union Khruschov slandered Stalin , abandoned the dicatorship of the proletariat and compromised with US imperialism . Socialism was crippled in the USSR , later it was finally destroyed from within by traitors like Gorbachov and Yeltsin . The same thing happened in a number of other countries. However had these countries being ideologically strong like the DPRK and had leaders like the great leader president Kim Il Sung , the great leader comrade Kim Jong Il and dear respected Marshal Kim Jong Un , then traitors like Gorbachov would have been exposed and destroyed ,so there would have no frustration of socialism in 1989-1991 and there would have been a 1 billion strong socialist camp standing in confrontation with imperialism. Indeed militant communists and true socialists are saying with a sigh , " *if only the USSR had been like the DPRK and Gorbachov*

had been purged ". The exposure and defeat of the counter-revolutionary Jang Song Thaek is a bold and decisive revolutionary measure taken by the dear respected leader Marshal Kim Jong Un . It is a great revolutionary victory that gives hope to the people of the world who aspire after socialism.
 The most dangerous enemy that a country and a party can face is the enemy within , the hidden unseen enemy that works ,hand in glove with the imperialists and class enemies , behind the scenes to frustrate and destroy socialism. The DPRK knows this lesson well but in other countries it was ignored. The DPRK under the Songun-based revolutionary leadership of dear respected Marshal Kim Jong Un is strong enough to defeat the enemy within.
 Some bourgeois so-called experts are prattling about "perestroika in reverse " , let these idiots prattle because "perestroika " was a complete disaster than destroyed socialism , a "reverse perestroika " will strengthen it. Cleansing the party and society of the counter-revolutionary factionalist gang will speed up socialist construction and strengthen the country. As the great leader president Kim Il Sung said
"All these traitors ended their days in misery. But did those revolutions get frustrated or retreat because of their betrayals? Each time the turncoats were removed, the revolution developed and surged up with fresh vitality. After the removal of Trotsky, how remarkably socialist construction was promoted in the Soviet Union! Trotsky thought that without him, everything Stalin did would fail, and the Soviet state would go to ruin. But the Soviet people built their country up to be the leading socialist power in the world, as well as a global power. After Zhang Guo-tao deserted the CPC and became a Kuo- mintang parasite, the Chinese revolution did not wane; on the contrary it continued its upward spiral and achieved nation-wide victory.

Though Rim Su San, after defecting to the enemy, divulged the secrets of our Headquarters and did us harm as a guide for the enemy "punitive" forces, the KPRA became neither weakened nor disrupted. Our ranks united more solidly and our revolution, preserving its own purity, made a strong dash towards its ultimate victory.

Traitors to the revolution also appeared during socialist construction in our country after the war. Choe Chang Ik, Yun Kong Hum, Ri Phil Gyu and others attempted to place obstacles in the way of our people's forward movement. Having failed to realize their factional scheme, they chose to betray the Party and their motherland. As they dropped away, our revolution made a fresh upsurge and ushered in the era of Chollima. Since then the world has called our country Chollima Korea."
(KIM IL SUNG "With the Century "
Now the counter-revolutionary traitor group has gone the DPRK will make a fresh surge forward under the banner of self-reliance, independence and Socialism under the intelligent leadership of dear respected Marshal Kim Jong Un.

Dermot Hudson
Chairman Juche Idea Study Group of England
President Association for the Study of Songun Politics

2.

Report on Enlarged Meeting of Political Bureau of Central Committee of WPK

Pyongyang, December 9 (KCNA) -- A report on the enlarged meeting of the Political Bureau of the Central Committee of the Workers' Party of Korea (WPK) was released on December 8.

The following is the full text of the report:

An enlarged meeting of the Political Bureau of the Central Committee of the WPK was held in

Pyongyang, the capital of the revolution, on Dec. 8.

Respected Comrade Kim Jong Un, first secretary of the WPK, guided the meeting.

Present there were members and alternate members of the Political Bureau of the Central Committee of the WPK.

Leading officials of the Central Committee of the WPK, provincial party committees and armed forces organs attended it as observers.

Our party members, service personnel and all other people have made energetic efforts to implement the behests of leader Kim Jong Il, entrusting their destiny entirely to Kim Jong Un and getting united close around the Central Committee of the WPK since the demise of Kim Jong Il, the greatest loss to the nation.

In this historic period for carrying forward the revolutionary cause of Juche the chance elements and alien elements who had made their ways into the party committed such anti-party, counter-revolutionary factional acts as expanding their forces through factional moves and daring challenge the party, while attempting to undermine the unitary leadership of the party.

In this connection, the Political Bureau of the C.C., the WPK convened its enlarged meeting and discussed the issue related to the anti-party, counter-revolutionary factional acts committed by Jang Song Thaek.

The meeting, to begin with, fully laid bare the anti-party, counter-revolutionary factional acts of Jang Song Thaek and their harmfulness and reactionary nature.

It is the immutable truth proved by the nearly 70-year-long history of the WPK that the party can preserve its revolutionary nature as the party of the leader and fulfill its historic mission only when it firmly ensures its unity and cohesion based on the monolithic idea and the unitary center of leadership.

The entire party, whole army and all people are dynamically advancing toward the final victory in the drive for the building of a thriving nation, meeting all challenges of history and resolutely foiling the desperate moves of the enemies of the revolution under the leadership of Kim Jong Un. Such situation urgently calls for consolidating as firm as a rock the single-minded unity of the party and the revolutionary ranks with Kim Jong Un as its unitary centre and more thoroughly establishing the monolithic leadership system of the party throughout the party and society.

The Jang Song Thaek group, however, committed such anti-party, counter-revolutionary factional acts as gnawing at the unity and cohesion of the party and disturbing the work for establishing the party unitary leadership system and perpetrated such ant-state, unpopular crimes as doing enormous harm to the efforts to build a thriving nation and improve the standard of people's living.

Jang pretended to uphold the party and leader but was engrossed in such factional acts as dreaming different dreams and involving himself in double-dealing behind the scene.

Though he held responsible posts of the party and state thanks to the deep political trust of the party and leader, he committed such perfidious acts as shunning and obstructing in every way the work for holding President Kim Il Sung and Kim Jong Il in high esteem for all ages, behaving against the elementary sense of moral obligation and conscience as a human being.

Jang desperately worked to form a faction within the party by creating illusion about him and winning those weak in faith and flatterers to his side.

Prompted by his politically-motivated ambition, he tried to increase his force and build his base for realizing it by implanting those who had been punished for their serious wrongs in the past period into ranks of officials of departments of the party central committee and units under them.

Jang and his followers did not sincerely accept the line and policies of the party, the organizational will of the WPK, but deliberately neglected their implementation, distorted them and openly played down the policies of the party. In the end, they made no scruple of perpetrating such counter-revolutionary acts as disobeying the order issued by the supreme commander of the Korean People's Army.

The Jang group weakened the party's guidance over judicial, prosecution and people's security bodies, bringing very harmful consequences to the work for protecting the social system, policies and people.

Such acts are nothing but counter-revolutionary, unpopular criminal acts of giving up the class struggle and paralyzing the function of popular democratic dictatorship, yielding to the offensive of the hostile forces to stifle the DPRK.

Jang seriously obstructed the nation's economic affairs and the improvement of the standard of people's living in violation of the pivot-to-the-Cabinet principle and the Cabinet responsibility principle laid down by the WPK.

The Jang group put under its control the fields and units which play an important role in the nation's economic development and the improvement of people's living in a crafty manner, making it impossible for the economic guidance organs including the Cabinet to perform their roles.

By throwing the state financial management system into confusion and committing such act of treachery as selling off precious resources of the country at cheap prices, the group made it impossible to carry out the behests of Kim Il Sung and Kim Jong Il on developing the industries of Juche iron, Juche fertilizer and Juche vinalon.

Affected by the capitalist way of living, Jang committed irregularities and corruption and led a dissolute and depraved life.

By abusing his power, he was engrossed in irregularities and corruption, had improper relations with several women and was wined and dined at back parlors of deluxe restaurants.

Ideologically sick and extremely idle and easy-going, he used drugs and squandered foreign currency at casinos while he was receiving medical treatment in a foreign country under the care of the party.

Jang and his followers committed criminal acts baffling imagination and they did tremendous harm to our party and revolution.

The ungrateful criminal acts perpetrated by the group of Jang Song Thaek are lashing our party members, service personnel of the People's Army and people into great fury as it committed such crimes before they observed two-year mourning for Kim Jong Il, eternal general secretary of the WPK.

Speeches were made at the enlarged meeting.

Speakers bitterly criticized in unison the anti-party, counter-revolutionary factional acts committed by the Jang group and expressed their firm resolution to remain true to the idea and leadership of Kim Jong Un and devotedly defend the Party Central Committee politically and ideologically and with lives.

The meeting adopted a decision of the Political Bureau of the Party Central Committee on relieving Jang of all posts, depriving him of all titles and expelling him and removing his name from the WPK.

The party served warning to Jang several times and dealt blows at him, watching his group's anti-party, counter-revolutionary factional acts as it has been aware of them from long ago. But it did not pay heed to it but went beyond tolerance limit. That was why the party eliminated Jang and purged his group, unable to remain an onlooker to its acts any longer, dealing telling blows at sectarian acts manifested within the party.

Our party will never pardon anyone challenging its leadership and infringing upon the interests of the state and people in violation of the principle of the revolution, regardless of his or her position and merits.

No matter how mischievously a tiny handful of anti-party, counter-revolutionary factional elements may work, they can never shake the revolutionary faith of all party members, service personnel and people holding Kim Jong Un in high esteem as the unitary centre of unity and unitary centre of leadership.

The discovery and purge of the Jang group, a modern day faction and undesirable elements who happened to worm their ways into our party ranks, made our party and revolutionary ranks purer and helped consolidate our single-minded unity remarkably and advance more dynamically the revolutionary cause of Juche along the road of victory.

No force on earth can deter our party, army and people from dynamically advancing toward a final victory, single-mindedly united around Kim Jong Un under the uplifted banner of great Kimilsungism-Kimjongilism.

Traitor Jang Song Thaek Executed

Pyongyang, December 13 (KCNA) -- Upon hearing the report on the enlarged meeting of the Political Bureau of the Central Committee of the Workers' Party of Korea, the service personnel and people throughout the country broke into angry shouts that a stern judgment of the revolution should be meted out to the anti-party, counter-revolutionary factional elements. Against the backdrop of these shouts rocking the country, a special military tribunal of the DPRK Ministry of State Security was held on December 12 against traitor for all ages Jang Song Thaek.

The accused Jang brought together undesirable forces and formed a faction as the boss of a modern day factional group for a long time and thus committed such hideous crime as attempting to overthrow the state by all sorts of intrigues and despicable methods with a wild ambition to grab the supreme power of our party and state.

The tribunal examined Jang's crimes.

All the crimes committed by the accused were proved in the course of hearing and were admitted by him.

A decision of the special military tribunal of the Ministry of State Security of the DPRK was read out at the trial.

Every sentence of the decision served as sledge-hammer blow brought down by our angry service personnel and people on the head of Jang, an anti-party, counter-revolutionary factional element and despicable political careerist and trickster.

The accused is a traitor to the nation for all ages who perpetrated anti-party, counter-revolutionary factional acts in a bid to overthrow the leadership of our party and state and the socialist system.

Jang was appointed to responsible posts of the party and state thanks to the deep political trust of President Kim Il Sung and leader Kim Jong Il and received benevolence from them more than any others from long ago.

He held higher posts than before and received deeper trust from supreme leader Kim Jong Un, in particular.

The political trust and benevolence shown by the peerlessly great men of Mt. Paektu were something he hardly deserved.

It is an elementary obligation of a human being to repay trust with sense of obligation and benevolence with loyalty.

However, despicable human scum Jang, who was worse than a dog, perpetrated thrice-cursed acts of treachery in betrayal of such profound trust and warmest paternal love shown by the party and the leader for him.

From long ago, Jang had a dirty political ambition. He dared not raise his head when Kim Il Sung and Kim Jong Il were alive. But, reading their faces, Jang had an axe to grind and involved himself in double-dealing. He began revealing his true colors, thinking that it was just the time for him to realize his wild ambition in the period of historic turn when the generation of the revolution was replaced.

Jang committed such an unpardonable thrice-cursed treason as overtly and covertly standing in the way of settling the issue of succession to the leadership with an axe to grind when a very important issue was under discussion to hold respected Kim Jong Un in high esteem as the only successor to Kim Jong Il in reflection of the unanimous desire and will of the entire party and army and all people.

When his cunning move proved futile and the decision that Kim Jong Un was elected vice-chairman of the Central Military Commission of the Workers' Party of Korea at the Third Conference of the WPK in reflection of the unanimous will of all party members, service personnel and people was proclaimed, making all participants break into enthusiastic cheers that shook the conference hall, he behaved so arrogantly and insolently as unwillingly standing up from his seat and half-heartedly clapping, touching off towering resentment of our service personnel and people.

Jang confessed that he behaved so at that time as a knee-jerk reaction as he thought that if Kim Jong Un's base and system for leading the army were consolidated, this would lay a stumbling block in the way of grabbing the power of the party and state.

When Kim Jong Il passed away so suddenly and untimely to our sorrow, he began working in real earnest to realize its long-cherished greed for power.

Abusing the honor of often accompanying Kim Jong Un during his field guidance, Jang tried hard to create illusion about him by projecting himself internally and externally as a special being on a par with the headquarters of the revolution.

In a bid to rally a group of reactionaries to be used by him for toppling the leadership of the party and state, he let the undesirable and alien elements including those who had been dismissed and relieved of their posts after being severely punished for disobeying the instructions of Kim Jong Il and kowtowing to him work in a department of the Central Committee of the WPK and organs under it in a crafty manner.

Jang did serious harm to the youth movement in our country, being part of the group of renegades and traitors in the field of youth work bribed by enemies. Even after they were disclosed and purged by the resolute measure of the party, he patronized those cat's paws and let them hold important posts of the party and state.

He had let Ri Ryong Ha, flatterer, work with him since the 1980s whenever he was transferred to other posts and systematically promoted Ri up to the post of first vice department director of the Party Central Committee though he had been purged for his factional act of denying the unitary leadership of the party. Jang thus made Ri his trusted stooge.

Jang let his confidants and flatterers who had been fired for causing an important case of denying the unitary leadership of the party work in his department and organs under it in a crafty manner in a few years. He systematically rallied ex-convicts, those problematic in their past careers and discontented elements around him and ruled over them as sacred and inviolable being.

He worked hard to put all affairs of the country under his control, massively increasing the staff of his department and organs under it, and stretch his tentacles to ministries and national institutions. He converted his department into a "little kingdom" which no one dares touch.

He was so imprudent as to prevent the Taedonggang Tile Factory from erecting a mosaic depicting Kim Il Sung and Kim Jong Il and a monument to field guidance given by them. Moreover, Jang turned down the unanimous request of the service personnel of a unit of the Korean People's Internal Security Forces to have the autograph letter sent by Kim Jong Un to the unit carved on a natural granite and erected with good care in front of the building of its command. He was so reckless as to instruct the unit to erect it in a shaded corner.

He committed such anti-party acts as systematically denying the party line and policies, its organizational will, in the past period. These acts were a revelation of deliberate and sinister attempt to create extreme illusion and idolization of him by making him appear as a special being who can overrule either issues decided by the party or its line.

He went so rude as to take in the middle even those things associated with intense loyalty and sincerity of our army and people towards the party and the leader and distribute them among his confidants in an effort to take credit upon himself for doing so. This behavior was to create illusion about him.

Due to his persistent moves to create illusion and idolization of him his flatterers and followers in his department and organs under it praised him as "No. 1 comrade." They went the lengths of denying even the party's instructions to please him at any cost.

Jang established such a heterogenous work system in the department and the relevant organs as considering what he said as more important than the party's policies. Consequently, his trusted henchmen and followers made no scruple of perpetrating such counterrevolutionary act as disobeying the order of the Supreme Commander of the KPA.

The revolutionary army will never pardon all those who disobey the order of the Supreme Commander and there will be no place for them to be buried even after their death.

Dreaming a fantastic dream to become premier at an initial stage to grab the supreme power of the party and state, Jang made his department put major economic fields of the country under its control in a bid to disable the Cabinet. In this way he schemed to drive the economy of the country and people's living into an uncontrollable catastrophe.

He put inspection and supervision organs belonging to the Cabinet under his control in defiance of the new state machinery established by Kim Jong Il at the First Session of the Tenth Supreme People's Assembly. He put all issues related to all structural works handled by the Cabinet under his control and had the final say on them, making it impossible for the Cabinet to properly perform its function and role as an economic command. They included the issues of setting up and disorganizing committees, ministries and national institutions and provincial, city and county-level organs, organizing units for foreign trade and earning foreign money and structures overseas and fixing living allowances.

When he attempted to make a false report to the party without having agreement with the Cabinet and the relevant ministry on the issue related to the state construction control organization, officials concerned expressed just opinion that his behavior was contrary to the construction law worked out by Kim Il Sung and Kim Jong Il. Hearing this, he made the reckless remark that "the rewriting of the construction law would solve the problem."

Abusing his authority, he undermined the work system related to the construction of the capital city established by Kim Il Sung and Kim Jong Il, reducing the construction building-materials bases to such bad shape little short of debris in a few years. He weakened the ranks of technicians and skilled workers at the unit for the construction of the capital city in a crafty manner and transferred major construction units to his confidants so that they might make money. In this way he deliberately disturbed the construction in Pyongyang.

He instructed his stooges to sell coal and other precious underground resources at random. Consequently, his confidants were saddled with huge debts, deceived by brokers. Jang made no scruple of committing such act of treachery in May last as selling off the land of the Rason economic and trade zone to a foreign country for a period of five decades under the pretext of paying those debts.

It was none other than Jang who wirepulled behind scene Pak Nam Gi, traitor for all ages, to recklessly issue hundreds of billions of won in 2009, sparking off serious economic chaos and disturbing the people's mind-set.

Jang encouraged money-making under various pretexts to secure funds necessary for gratifying his political greed and was engrossed in irregularities and corruption. He thus took the lead in spreading indolent, careless and undisciplined virus in our society.

After collecting rare metals since the construction of Kwangbok Street in the 1980s, he set up a secret organ under his control and took a fabulous amount of funds from a bank and purchased rare metals in disregard of the state law. He thus committed such anti-state criminal acts as creating a great confusion in financial management system of the state.

He let the decadent capitalist lifestyle find its way to our society by distributing all sorts of pornographic pictures among his confidants since 2009. He led a dissolute, depraved life, squandering money wherever he went.

He took at least 4.6 million Euro from his secret coffers and squandered it in 2009 alone and enjoyed himself in casino in a foreign country. These facts alone clearly show how corrupt and degenerate he was.

Jang was so reckless with his greed for power that he persistently worked to stretch his tentacles even to the People's Army with a foolish calculation that he would succeed in staging a coup if he mobilized the army.

He fully revealed his despicable true colors as a traitor for all ages in the course of questioning by uttering as follows: "I attempted to trigger off discontent among service personnel and people when the present regime does not take any measure despite the fact that the economy of the country and people's living are driven into catastrophe. Comrade supreme leader is the target of the coup."

As regards the means and methods for staging the coup, Jang said: "I was going to stage the coup by using army officers who had close ties with me or by mobilizing armed forces under the control of my confidants. I don't know well about recently appointed army officers but have some acquaintances with those appointed in the past period. I thought the army might join in the coup if the living of the people and service personnel further deteriorate in the future. And I calculated that my confidants in my department including Ri Ryong Ha and Jang Su Gil would surely follow me and had a plan to use the one in charge of the people's security organ as my confidant. It was my calculation that I might use several others besides them."

Asked about the timing of the coup and his plan to do after staging the coup, Jang answered: "I didn't fix the definite time for the coup. But it was my intention to concentrate my department and all economic organs on the Cabinet and become premier when the economy goes totally bankrupt and the state is on the verge of collapse in a certain period. I thought that if I solve the problem of people's living at a certain level by spending an enormous amount of funds I have accumulated under various names after becoming premier, the people and service personnel will shout "hurrah" for me and I will succeed in the coup in a smooth way."

Jang dreamed such a foolish dream that once he seizes power by a base method, his despicable true colors as "reformist" known to the outside world would help his "new government" get "recognized" by foreign countries in a short span of time.

All facts go to clearly prove that Jang is a thrice-cursed traitor without an equal in the world as he had desperately worked for years to destabilize and bring down the DPRK and grab the supreme power of the party and state by employing all the most cunning and sinister means and methods, pursuant to the "strategic patience" policy and "waiting strategy" of the U.S. and the south Korean puppet group of traitors.

The hateful and despicable nature of the anti-party, anti-state and unpopular crimes committed by Jang was fully disclosed in the course of the trial conducted at the special military tribunal of the DPRK Ministry of State Security.

The era and history will eternally record and never forget the shuddering crimes committed by Jang Song Thaek, the enemy of the party, revolution and people and heinous traitor to the nation.

No matter how much water flows under the bridge and no matter how frequently a generation is replaced by new one, the lineage of Paektu will remain unchanged and irreplaceable.

Our party, state, army and people do not know anyone except Kim Il Sung, Kim Jong Il and Kim Jong Un.

Our service personnel and people will never pardon all those who dare disobey the unitary leadership of Kim Jong Un, challenge his absolute authority and oppose the lineage of Paektu to an individual but bring them to the stern court of history without fail and mercilessly punish them on behalf of the party and revolution, the country and its people, no matter where they are in hiding.

The special military tribunal of the Ministry of State Security of the DPRK confirmed that the state subversion attempted by the accused Jang with an aim to overthrow the people's power of the DPRK by ideologically aligning himself with enemies is a crime punishable by Article 60 of the DPRK Criminal Code, vehemently condemned him as a wicked political careerist, trickster and traitor for all ages in the name of the revolution and the people and ruled that he would be sentenced to death according to it.

The decision was immediately executed

STATEEMENTS OF ASSPUK ,JISGE AND UK KFA

ASSPUK, JISGE and UK KFA on defeat of counter-revolution in Juche Korea !

London 8th of December Juche 102(2013)
 On hearing that the news that the Political Bureau of the Workers' Party of Korea had decided to expel Jang Song Thaek for counter-revolutionary acts, we the JISGE, ASSPUK and UK KFA resolved to issue the following statement ;
 The ASSPUK , JISGE and UK KFA fully support the measures taken by the Political Bureau of the Workers' Party of Korea, at its enlarged meeting on 8th of December , against the counter-revolutionary factional clique of the traitor Jang Song Thaek . We congratulate dear respected Marshal Kim Jong Un and the Workers' Party of Korea on the timely defeat of the counter-revolution in the DPRK , the bastion of true socialism.
 The most dangerous enemy a country and a party can face is the enemy within , the unseen hidden enemy that is hand in glove with imperialism and class enemies . It shows the strength of the Korean revolution that this traitor was exposed and defeated !
 Those who aimed to smash up Juche socialism and turn the DPRK a colony of imperialism or a

satellite state of another country have now been defeated. We believe that under the Songun-based revolutionary leadership of dear respected Marshal Kim Jong Un , the people will unite even more strongly than before and deal blows to the enemies of Juche . We believe that under the banners of Songun , independence, self-reliance and socialism that the Korean revolution will win victory after victory !

LONG LIVE DEAR RESPECTED MARSHAL KIM JONG UN!
LONG LIVE KIMILSUNGISM-KIMJONGILISM !

ASSPUK
JISGE
UK KFA

ASSPUK and JISGE on execution of counter-revolutionary traitor Jang

13th December Juche 102(2013)

 On hearing the news of the execution of traitor Jang Song Thaek the Association for the Study of Songun Politics UK and Juche Idea Study Group of England decided to issue the following joint statement;
 It is entirely just that the Korean people should execute Jang Song Thaek the traitor for all ages .
The special military tribunal of the Ministry of State Security laid bare the profoundly grave crimes of Jang which not only included treason and counter-revolutionary intrigue but extreme corruption and degeneration. It is now apparent that for ages Jang was sabotaging the DPRK economy causing big losses to the country and impeding the improvement of the people's living standards . This is a crime that cannot go unpunished and can only be punished most severely.
Jang was a capitalist roader who planned to destroy Juche-based socialism and restore capitalism in the DPRK. Jang was ideologically aligned to US imperialism and the south Korean puppets.   As the verdict of the Special military tribunal says "*Jang dreamed such a foolish dream that once he seizes power by a base method, his despicable true colors as "reformist" known to the outside world would help his "new government" get "recognized" by foreign countries in a short span of time"*.
"Reform " and "opening " mean surrendering to imperialism and restoring capitalism. Capitalism would cause great suffering to the people with many thrown out of work and driven to suicide .
This could never be allowed to happen.Never !
Athough some revisionists and fake leftists may shed tears for Jang the fact is that his execution is a just revolutionary measure that has stopped the enemies of Juche socialism in their tracks. If only the USSR had taken the same measures against the internal traitors , socialism would still exist in the USSR. We in the ASSPUK and JISGE fully recognise that under socialism class struggle against the enemies of people goes on . We see the measures taken against Jang within the context of the severe class struggle against imperialism and class enemies. It should not be seen otherwise.
 Now that capitalist roader and counter -revolutionary filth has been
cleansed from the DPRK socialist construction will go ahead with greater strength under the banner of Kimilsungism-Kimjongilism under the wise
leadership of dear respected Marshal Kim Jong Un !

LONG LIVE DEAR RESPECTED MARSHAL KIM JONG UN!
LONG LIVE DPRK !
DEATH TO COUNTER-REVOLUTION

ASSPUK
JISGE

UK KFA on the Jang Affair and FCO Interference in the DPRK

15th of December

The Korean people have now exposed, purged and physically liquidated the corrupt traitor Jang Song Thaek who had betrayed the country. However the reactionary British Foreign and Commonwealth Office and some right wing British politicians decided to take issue with it .

UK KFA firmly declares firstly, that it is no business of the British government to interfere in an internal affair of the DPRK , it is the business of the DPRK alone who is punished and the form of punishment used , it is not the business of Britain , the US or any other country . Secondly, the British government did not worry when Col Gadhafi or Saddam Hussein were killed, they cheered when this happened. Thirdly, it did not worry when hundreds of thousands died in wars in which Britain participated , nor did they worry about the 'shoot to kill' policy in northern Ireland nor when British troops killed civilians in Derry city in 1972. The FCO only worries about the execution of one person in the DPRK .

The execution of the traitor Jang Song Thaek was a just and correct measure. Jang was not only a counter-revolutionary who planned to overthrow the people-centred socialist system but was extremely corrupt . He not only stole money from the state and gambled it away but was even sold off land that did not belong to him. He damaged the independent economy of the DPRK by selling off goods at cheap prices to foreign countries . Thus Jang caused enormous losses to the Korean people so it would be unreasonable to expect the DPRK to imprison him and fed him at state expense . Moreover Jang had been warned many times , he had been given many chances. Given his age it would be unlikely that he would change his ways.

jang had planned to stage a coup to overthrow the supreme leadership of the DPRK , it is improbable that such a coup would be not be bloodless but would cost lives . Thus the swift and resolute action of the WPK Poltical Bureau and the Special Military Tribunal of the Ministry of State Security maintained stablity and saved many lives which otherwise would have been lost in a Jang inspired coup.

Jang planned to restore capitalism in the DPRK and turn into a satellite state of another country as well as selling out to US imperialism. As is well known the dismantlement of the socialist system in the former USSR and other socialist countries caused immense misery and suffering to the peoples of those countries. Respected Marshal Kim Jong Un and the WPK were determined that this should not be repeated in the DPRK .

The measures taken by the Political Bureau of the Workers' Party of Korea and the DPRK Ministry of State Security actually show the strength of people-centred Juche-based socialism. It shows that corruption is dealt with firmly and robustly in the DPRK . In the UK corrupt members of parliament who fiddled expenses mostly got away with it with only a tinyhandful being imprisoned and those that were imprisoned were just imprisoned for a maximum of 18 months. The action taken shows that the DPRK is people-centred democracy , a proletarian democracy that does not allow corruption.

Jang's liquidation was an expression of the will of the Korean people-soldiers , workers and others had all demanded that he put to death. It is not for Whitehall mandarins and overpaid parliamentarians to interfere in this. UK KFA believes the people's justice had been done .

UK KFA

APPENDIX
a) Letter to the Morning Star
Dear Sir
The article "Schism in North Korea " was without a doubt one of the worst articles
ever to appear in the "Morning Star " . The "Star " has truly crossed the Rubicon. It has degenerated from being a
revisionist newspaper to being an openly pro-imperialist , anti-communist and social democratic . The editorial

rehashed the lies of the capitalist press with a few cheap throwaway jibes aiming at currying favour with Trotskyites .
The article read like a mixture of the "Sun" newspaper and the "Socialist Worker " on a bad day .
The defeat of the counter-revolutionary faction in the DPRK should be a matter for congratulation , all communists ,
socialists and anti-imperialists should be
supporting it . The swift , decisive and resolute action taken by Marshal Kim Jong Un
has dealt a blow to the imperialists , as shown by the comments made by the reactionary Lord Alton of
Liverpool that J ang Song Thaek was a "real hope for reform " in the DPRK . It is more than the class
enemy is angry about the elimination of its agent in the DPRK but why should the "Star" a supposedly
"socialist daily newspaper " join hands with them in attacking the DPRK.
Had the USSR and CPSU taken similar decisive measures against Gorbachov and Yeltsin socialism was still
exist in the USSR today , this is a fact.
All the old lies of the capitalist media about the DPRK are spewed up by the "Morning Star ". Rather than
living standards declining in the DPRK they are improving as a large number of leisure and cultural
facilities have been built in the DPRK in the past 18 months. Education and health care are free in the
DPRK , housing is virtually free and people do not pay tax. The Pyongyang Metro is the cheapest in the
world only 2.5p for the fare
and a 1 litre bottle of beer in the DPRK is 20p . What is this , if is not socialism ?
The "Morning Star " sides with imperialism in calling for the overthrow of the socialist system in the DPRK.
No doubt this will win the "Star " some new friends.
However there is no schism in the DPRK , a handful of counter-revolutionary factionalists do not represent
anyone. The people are solidly united around the party and the leader.
        yours etc
Dermot Hudson

Refutation of attack on the DPRK by the British modern revisionists-an unofficial commentary

The "Morning Star " , which is a faded version of the old "Daily Worker " of Britain (the
revisionists changed the name from "Daily Worker " to "Morning Star " in order to distance
themselves from the working class and militant communism) , in an editorial attacked the supreme
leadership of the DPRK and slandered the socialist system of the DPRK .

The article " Schism in north Korea " seems to be a mixture of the "Sun" newspaper and quasi
Trotskyite rantings . The "Morning Star" just repeats the lies of the capitalist media about

"starvation " etc . The supposedly left wing newspaper seems to share the concern of imperialism that counter-revolution in the DPRK has been smashed and effectively calls for a counter revolution in the DPRK. We cannot help wondering whether the south Korean puppet embassy slipped the "Morning Star " a few backhanders to print such rubbish about the DPRK ?

The following comments can be made of the article ;
 Firstly, there is no schism in the DPRK , it is ridiculous to style a handful of traitors , counter-revolutionary factionalists , a schism . The people are united firmly around supreme leader comrade Kim Jong Un and the Workers' Party of Korea . Moreover the traitor was not the "number two " in the leadership , this in an invention of the capitalist press and some so-called "Korea experts " (who are in reality in the pay of south Korea and the US) . The socialist system of the DPRK is a people - centred socialist system of a Korean -style and will not perish. It has survived despite the sanctions and blockades of US imperialism and its followers and all the pressure that they put on it . The DPRK has foiled attempts by the south Korean puppet regime to subvert and destroy by means of terrorism etc . The fact that the anti-party counter-revolutionary faction was smashed and defeated actually shows the strength of the socialist system of the DPRK.

 Secondly, dear respected Marshal Kim Jong Un and the Workers' Party of Korea should be praised for their swift , resolute and decisive action against the counter-revolution . Had the USSR taken such resolute and decisive measures against Gorbachov, Yeltsin , socialism in the USSR would not have collapsed .

Thirdly , it was the demand of the Korean people that the traitor be executed. Meetings of soldiers and workers demanded that the traitor be put to death. The execution was an expression of the peoples will and people's justice which is different to bourgeois justice . It was people's democracy, proletarian democracy in action.

 Fourthly, the "Morning Star " resorts to "Sun " and "Daily Mail " lies and slanders against the DPRK . The 'starvation ' stories have been proved time and time again to be myths but the "Star " rakes them up . Basketball is not simply the personal taste of the supreme leader but is immensely popular with the whole people , as shown in the famous DPRK film " A Family Basketball Team" The "Morning Star " even goes as far to say that living standards are declining in the DPRK when in fact they are going up . In recent years numerous large scale cultural and service facilities have been constructed in the DPRK such as the Rungna People's Pleasure Park, Munsu Water Park , Ryugyong Health Complex one after the other as well new health care institutions such as the Ryugyong Dental Hospital , Okryu Childrens Hospital and the Breast Tumour Institute of the Pyongyang Maternity Hospital . Even the DPRK enemies were compelled to admit that the DPRK was growing faster than south Korea (Businessweek 30 June 2009) and this year was according to some financial newspapers is growing faster than Brazil . The foolish "Morning Star " ignores these facts . In the DPRK housing is virtually free of charge and health and education are free of charge.Prices are low it is only the equivalent of 2.5p to use the Pyongyang Metro.

 Fifth , the " Star " is factually inaccurate , the traitor was never accused of trying to form his 'own dynasty' but of trying to create his own empire within the WPK "He worked hard to put all affairs of the country under his control, massively increasing the staff of his department and organs under it, and stretch his tentacles to ministries and national institutions. He converted his department into a "little kingdom" which no one dares touch.". In other words he was an arrogant big boss figure.

Sixth, the "Morning Star " deliberately distorts the essence of Songun politics. In the DPRK the people's armed forces are under the leadership and guidance of the Workers' Party of Korea . As the dear respected Marshal Kim Jong Un said
" *Leadership of the Party is the lifeline of the KPA, and its might is inconceivable separated from the leadership of the Party. The general direction ahead of the KPA is one, that is, to advance straight forward with guns levelled in the very direction our Party indicates. Our arms must serve as an ever-lasting cornerstone that ensures a sure guarantee for the Party and its cause.*" **"Let Us Add Eternal Brilliance to Comrade Kim Jong Il's Great Idea and Achievements of the Songun Revolution*"* 25 August 2013).
If you see military parades in the DPRK you will see the gold and red flag of the Workers' Party of Korea displayed by army units and fluttering proudly on the top of military vehicles .
Basically Songun politics is fundamentally different from military governments in capitalist countries. The former is a democratic mode of socialist politics administered for the sake of the people, while the latter is an anti-popular, fascist mode of politics as the consequence of capitalist crisis.This difference is rooted in that in ideology and ideal. Songun politics, guided by the Juche idea which advocates the independence of the masses of the people and countries and nations, can never be compatible with the mode of politics administered by military regimes or fascist dictators based on misanthropy and national chauvinism. The DPRK has given top priority to military affairs and highlighted the role of its army, proceeding solely from the interests of its people and its specific conditions. In other words, Korea has staunchly followed the road of sovereignty, independence and socialism in confrontation with imperialist powers and, in the course of this, the traditions of attaching importance to military affairs were created and eventually the mode of Songun politics has been established in all aspects of life. The Songun idea and Songun politics are essential for the DPRK which is in direct confrontation with US imperialism and the south Korean puppets. The guns of the US army are levelled at the DPRK and it is targeted by nuclear bombs . No doubt the "Morning Star " editor ensconced in a cosy office thinks that the DPRK can defend itself by waving flowers and saying "peaceful co-existence ".

All in all the "Morning Star " editorial is an extreme slander on the DPRK that simply replicates the attacks of the bourgeois and imperialist media on the DPRK and its supreme leadership , the article would not be out of place in the "Independent " or "Guardian " or even the "Daily Mail ". "Schism in north Korea " is a grave disservice of the traditions of the "Daily Worker " which defended the socialist countries and supported the DPRK in the Korean war. Now they have stooped lower than the lowest .

A former "Morning Star " reader and supporter.